The
BOOK
of
Common
Courage

K.J. RAMSEY

PRAYERS AND POEMS
TO FIND STRENGTH IN
SMALL MOMENTS

 ZONDERVAN

ZONDERVAN

The Book of Common Courage

© 2023 Katie Jo Ramsey

Published in Grand Rapids, Michigan, by Zondervan. Zondervan is a registered trademark of The Zondervan Corporation, L.L.C., a wholly owned subsidiary of HarperCollins Christian Publishing, Inc.

Requests for information should be addressed to customercare@harpercollins.com.

ISBN 978-0-3104-6136-4 (audiobook)
ISBN 978-0-3104-6130-2 (eBook)
ISBN 978-0-3104-6133-3 (HC)

All photography courtesy of K.J. Ramsey.

Art direction: Tiffany Forrester

Interior design: Emily Ghattas

Cover design and illustration: © Conrad Garner

Printed in the United States of America

23 24 25 26 27 VER 6 5 4 3 2

To all who do not
believe you are brave

CONTENTS

PART 3: GIVEN

Coolio quoted Psalm 23.

In 1995 the biggest record of the year was by hip-hop artist Coolio with his song "Gangsta's Paradise." At a time when there weren't streaming services, I remember listening to the radio constantly for it to play, just trying to catch some part of that haunting tune with the catchy Los Angeles street lyrics that somehow seemed to resonate with this artsy Pacific Northwest Seattle kid. The song is magic all the way through, and even if we trip up on some of the lyrics throughout the song, not one of us will ever forget how it starts:

"As I walk through the valley of the shadow of death."

That line. Isn't it amazing that a line, penned by someone thousands of years ago describing what the darkest days of their human life looked like, still deeply resonates with our modern lives today? And it's not only that line in this psalm, but all the lines in this psalm, in my experience, seem to draw us into a deeply personal and yet universal experience of our remembrance, yearning, and hope of God in the midst of a complicated life.

Psalm 23 was the first large piece of Scripture I ever memorized. I've known it for years and have recited it to myself an unknown amount of times. Even though I'm exhaustingly familiar with it, I still find it deeply excavating to the life I find myself showing up to day after day. I think it's because, as a visual artist, I find the visual imagery so poignantly rich. A providing shepherd. Green pastures. Quiet waters. Renewed souls.

Dark valleys. Tables of provision. Oil anointing. Cup overflowing. Holy houses. Dwelling forever. These shapes, spaces, and settings mentioned in this ancient song are evergreen to the conversations, whispers, prayers, and pleas of the pilgrim today.

If I'm honest, I don't think I've ever read these words and thought, *I wonder what it's like to be that guy?* From the first time I read them, I always assumed they were a description of my life. I've never even thought that these words were about anyone else's life other than my own. That's how powerful they are. That's why Scripture is so poignant. It's not just a story that's happening back then. It's a story that's happening right now. Psalm 23 has become the autobiographical prayer of so many of us, whether we're walking the streets of ancient Jerusalem or cruising downtown Los Angeles.

In the same tradition of illuminating how this story is still happening today, K.J. invites us to excavate our lives with Psalm 23 in the pages before you. Sometimes we know how to do this on our own, but sometimes it's helpful to have a friend along the way to offer us the meditations, questions, and invitations to a transformed perspective. She's a trusted guide and a seasoned pilgrim with much to offer us in the contemplation of these words.

My prayer is that you would find, like I and many others have, that the words of Psalm 23 are not just a song to sing but a reality to awaken ourselves to.

SCOTT ERICKSON, AUTHOR OF *HONEST ADVENT*

When I was finishing writing this book, my life shrunk. An infection—that we belatedly learned was Covid-19—became chaos in my immunocompromised body, and my life became as small as my queen-sized bed. As days turned into weeks, my prayers became pleas.

Help. Please. Heal.

But after three infections, two rounds of antibiotics, and a month of fever and debilitating fatigue, I was losing my grip on hope. I couldn't see a way out of the dark valley of illness, and even my pleading, one-word prayers were turning into silence. The prayer book author couldn't pray.

When we feel small and stuck, it's hard to summon words. What I know as a licensed therapist is that when harm happens or life hurts too much for too long, our bodies temporarily shut down to survive, disconnecting us from our brains' innate capacity to name and tame the truth of our experiences. When stress surges through our bodies like a raging storm, words tend to get lost in the wind.

When we cannot find the words to pray, we are not faithless. We are feeling the fact that we are both embodied and vulnerable.

I was referred to an endocrinologist out of concern that a rare disorder I'd had years before was back, chaining me to bed. Showing up to my initial virtual appointment felt like my boldest remaining prayer. All I could do was dare to trust that letting this woman see how sick I was wouldn't just bring more silence.

My husband sat next to me on our bed, holding my hand

while I struggled to hold up my body, propped up against our orange pillow shams as we waited for Dr. R. to pop up on my computer screen. When there's a good chance a doctor might not believe I'm as sick as I am, Ryan comes with me, ready to advocate when I feel flooded by the pent-up anxiety of years of disbelief.

It took all the energy I had to explain why I needed help, how bathing became my biggest accomplishment in a day and walking the fifteen steps to our bathroom required an hour of rest. "I *can't* take this anymore." I heaved my final explanation out with a sudden burst of tears, protesting what my life had become.

When I looked back up, Dr. R. had tears in her eyes.

"This is a physical low point in your life," she said, "but *you will get better.*"

She went on to explain how I almost definitely had adrenal insufficiency, the disorder I had faced and recovered from before, how I needed replacement cortisol therapy and physical therapy, how it would not be a quick recovery and there likely would be more issues to uncover, but that I *would* recover. But it was her first response to my story and tears that brought hope near.

Her words were like a benediction. *A blessing.*

I grew up in a little Presbyterian church, where at the end of every Sunday service we'd raise our hands like sunflowers to the sky, open-palmed to receive our pastor's benediction.

The LORD bless you
and keep you;

the LORD make his face shine on you
and be gracious to you;
the LORD turn his face toward you
and give you peace.[1]

I remember the day I realized that opening my hands mattered, that I wasn't just mimicking the adults; I was letting goodness reach me right where I was.

As Jesus prepared his closest friends for the days their hopes would be dashed, he told them, "In this world you will have trouble. But take heart! I have overcome the world."[2]

"But take heart!" can also be translated as "Be courageous!"[3] When Jesus told his friends how to find strength when trouble comes, he told them that courage is a matter of holding the heart. He didn't say, "Take mind!" He didn't say, "Take thought!" He said, "*Take heart.*"

When my doctor looked into my eyes and said I would get better, she reached toward my heart. She spoke into the space between my hurt and my healing and hallowed it as hope-filled ground. Her words blessed me back into belief that there would be goodness ahead for me.

To bless is to bridge. A blessing is a bridge to belonging, built right in the place we feel separated from hope. Words of blessing bring us back to the beautiful truth of being human: we belong to one another, and it is in the space between our souls that we become strong.

When life makes us feel stuck, scared, or small, the storms of stress separate our minds from our bodies and hearts and ourselves from one another. Fear can turn our hands to fists and our feet to flight. We sink into overwhelm and shut down in storms of stress in an effort to survive, but rushing and retreating aren't exactly the path to strength and joy.

It's hard to pray when we feel powerless because our bodies need the presence of someone else to soothe us and speak us back into safety. Fear and stress temporarily disconnect us from the language centers of the brain and the calming, regulating power of the prefrontal cortex, but the presence of another safe, empathetic person can bring our minds, bodies, and hearts back together.

A fourteenth-century definition of courage is "to speak one's mind by telling all of one's heart."[4] Courage is connecting one's heart back to one's mind, stitching together the separated parts of ourselves and one another. Courage is holding the heart when the mind can't hope.

I titled this collection of prayers and poems *The Book of Common Courage* because courage is something we hold in common. Courage is not the possession of the bravest or biggest but the choice to move toward the heart when the mind and body are separated by fear. Courage is the choice to move our fear into communion.

When we don't have words, we need a witness. We need with-ness.

When we find ourselves struggling to be strong in yet another dark valley of vulnerability, we need to sense there is a Shepherd coming to care for us. This book follows the familiar path of Psalm 23 word by word and phrase by phrase to welcome us back into our truest story.

Courage isn't the opposite of fear. *Courage is the practice of trusting we have a Good Shepherd who always cares—even when vulnerability is shouting otherwise.*[5]

These words are my small witness to your life, my withness to your weariness, and my welcome back to the home of your heart. Within these pages you will find prayers, poems, and some blessings to bridge the space between your pain and God's promises.

Sometimes suffering shifts the beams of our belonging. Harm and hurt can make old ways of worship sting like open wounds. And when prayer becomes painful or the Word of God is clouded with question marks, we might wonder whether we belong in the body of Christ anymore.

At the end of my twenties, my husband and I were waking up to the heart-shattering reality that we were part of a spiritually abusive faith community, a story I shared in much more detail in the book that inspired this one, *The Lord Is My Courage*. The Word of God had been used against us like a weapon. People who were supposed to shepherd us cut against our character, sense of reality, and hope with the sword of sharp words and subtle gaslighting. After we left, we felt like we were lost in a wilderness. The only prayers that made sense were the imprecatory prayers of the psalmists. Trauma shattered our safety and trust, and stepping inside the doors of a church brought on panic attacks. The safety and strength I once received with open palms from my childhood pastor's benedictions now seemed shrouded, left behind under the loss of our community.

When we don't have a witness and we lose our with-ness, we struggle to see the Word-become-flesh is still with us.

I needed new ways to see there was still a Good Shepherd coming to care for me. I needed new language for old love, speech that was safe and strong enough to hold my suffering and touch my trauma. Eventually, through therapy, time, and practice, my husband and I found both our words and communal worship again. We've spent the last few years healing in a small liturgical church, where I've learned to let the form and rhythm of liturgy lift me.

I've grown to love *The Book of Common Prayer* and its collects. A collect, pronounced *kahl-ect*, is a brief form of prayer that distills our desires down to the most needful thing. Each week in our church we pray collects, including the familiar words of the collect for purity:

> Almighty God, to you all hearts are open, all desires known, and from you no secrets are hid: Cleanse the thoughts of our hearts by the inspiration of your Holy Spirit, that we may perfectly love you, and worthily magnify your holy Name; through Christ our Lord. Amen.[6]

A collect has a cadence and a concentration aimed at communion. In the overwhelm of my own wilderness, I've found comfort in the simplicity and structure of collects.

You have two lungs and one heart. As with breath and beat, the form of rhythm is what makes us rise. Prayer can be a rhythm of returning back home. Prayer can gather up our fear-filled bodies and weary hearts with words that remind us we are not alone. When it is hard to pray and hard to hope, we do not have to try harder to pray ourselves from fear to faith. We can enter the rhythm of others' prayers. We can let a form of prayer hold us as we journey back to strength.

I've included collects in every chapter of this book to give us structured space to be held. The origin of the word *collect* comes from the early fifteenth century, meaning "to gather into one place or group."[7] A collect can give us words to be gathered up in our grief and contained and embraced in the midst of fear or stress that seems uncontainable.

Like the familiar collect for purity, the collects in this book tuck our prayers into five folds.[8]

1. **We name God.** We begin talking with God by naming God.
2. **We name the story or character of God.** We name part of the story of God or attributes of God.
3. **We name our desire.** We choose just one desire, one want.
4. **We name our why.** We share the reason we want what we want, echoing the name and story of God.
5. **We praise.** We end with an amen or a small word of praise.

When our stories are unfolding in ways we probably would not have written, we can feel out of sorts. As a trauma-informed therapist, I believe that when our nervous systems are flooded by stress, *less is more*. The brevity of a collect can bridge us back to strength in a few words, rather than overstimulating ourselves with long prayers.

The Irish poet Pádraig Ó Tuama calls the collect "a haiku of intention."[9] The prayers and poems in this book might feel simpler than you expect, and that is on purpose. From simple collect prayers, to approachable poems, to photos from my surroundings, I have gathered words and images meant to bless our smallness and small moments into strength. My intent is that we encounter even the fragile and flooded parts of ourselves as welcome in prayer and gathered up by Christ in God.

If we are honest, sometimes in small moments of stress and big seasons of suffering, God can seem like an absent or apathetic Father. In Christ, God has a face and footsteps. In Christ, we can see God's gaze turned toward the weak and the weary—turned toward us.

While many of the collects in *The Book of Common Prayer* are addressed to God the Father and end in a Trinitarian formula of blessing the Father, Son, and Spirit, I've chosen to direct many of the collects in this book to Jesus, to welcome us into conversation with the promised Good Shepherd of Psalm 23. Instead of lofty language, I wrote like I talk. Many of the collects are paired with scriptures that show us our Shepherd in action—as fully human, speaking with his friends, feeding the hungry, and seeking those whom religious society was content to forget.

The first person in Scripture to name God was Hagar—a woman, abused and traumatized, and far from help and home.[10]

In these collects, like Hagar, we get to name God. We, the help-less and hopeless. We, the harmed. We, the hurting. *We* get to name God and name our desires right in the places we feel powerless and small.

Christ emptied himself and became as human as you and me so every part of our humanity could be lived in his pres-ence. Emptiness precedes presence. And courage is the practice of coming to the empty space where heart and mind struggle to meet, expecting to encounter the Good Shepherd emptying himself and embracing us even still.

I like to think of prayer like a singing bowl, a type of small metal bowl that many have used in meditation and prayer for centuries. Slowly, one circles the edge of the empty bowl with a mallet until the bowl sings. It takes practice. It takes patience. But held and encircled with care, the bowl can sing.

Just as in an unfilled singing bowl, a song can rise out of our emptiness as we trace the circle of our hard days and moments with the patience of prayer. When we are emptied of strength, there still can be a song.

Just as I found myself in yet another season of sickness while finishing this book, Psalm 23 situates us in a song that repeats itself. The psalm itself is written in a literary form called a *ring composition*, in which the psalmist, David, reflected on aspects of our relationship with God by telling a story to its climax and then repeating the story backwards with a slight variation.[11]

Psalm 23 is a circle, and courage is too. When we find ourselves in another hard, dark valley, we are still in the circle of God's care. In small moments, when our strength has shrunk yet again and words are hard to find, we are still in the story where a Shepherd seeks us.

Courage is a practice, and prayer is too. These collects, poems, and blessings are a bridge I've built for you to encounter the compassionate presence of our Good Shepherd. Make them your own. Mark in the margins. Replace my words with ones that resonate with you more. Try following the five folds of a collect to write your own.

However you engage with this book, I pray that in these words you will trace the edge of your life. I pray you will choose to bless rather than curse your emptiness and approach your life with curiosity rather than control.

Even that which confounds us can be a container for communion.

An empty bowl can sing.

And, strangely, your cup will overflow.

The LORD is my SHEPHERD, I Lack NOTHING.
HE Makes ME LIE down IN GREEN Pastures,
HE Leads ME BESIDE QUIET WATERS,
he REFRESHES my SOUL.
HE GUIDES ME along the RIGHT Paths
for his NAME'S SAKE. EVEN THOUGH I WALK
through THE DARKEST VALLEY, I will FEAR NO EVIL.
FOR you ARE WITH me;
YOUR ROD and YOUR STAFF, They COMFORT ME.
you Prepare a TABLE before ME in the PRESENCE
of MY ENEMIES. YOU ANOINT MY Head with OIL;
MY CUP OVERFLOWS.
Surely YOUR GOODNESS and Love will FOLLOW ME
ALL THE Days of MY Life,
AND I will DWELL in THE House
OF the LORD FOREVER.

PSALM 23 NIV

PART

I

BLESSED

In those days Jesus came from Nazareth of Galilee and was baptized by John in the Jordan. And just as he was coming up out of the water, he saw the heavens torn apart and the Spirit descending like a dove on him. And a voice came from the heavens, "You are my Son, the Beloved; with you I am well pleased."

MARK 1:9-11 NRSV

Lord Jesus,

who stepped down
onto the muddy banks
of the Jordan where
your cousin John

pulled you under

to be drenched in the baptism
of a repentance God surely didn't need
so that every waterlogged ear
could be freed to rise to the sound
of the Voice of Love coming down:

we want to hear
what you heard
that strange day.

Because though
we call you Lord
we forget to call
ourselves
Beloved.

But your ears
still hear
the words
that seem
drowned out:

we are God's Beloved

through the Spirit, in you,
Christ, God's Son.

Amen.

What is your only comfort
to be courageous
in life and in death?

That everywhere I go, I belong
—body and soul, in all my days,
all my doubts, and even
all my despair,
and my coming death—
to you, my Savior
and my friend, Jesus Christ.

Lord Jesus,
there is nothing in life
and no manner of death
that can separate me
from your friendship.

Everywhere I go,
you go with me.
You are always glad
to be with me.

Because you became like me,
I can become like you.

Because you felt
fear, anger, and betrayal,
even in my anguish,
I can partake of your life.

Because you were faithful to feel
and trust,
even in my fear,
I can be faithful too.

Your trust in the Father
to work goodness and life
re-creates my own.

Your courage in the face of death
has made the Father mine,
the Spirit present,
and my future secure.

You have fully paid
for all my sins and all my debts,
with the precious currency
of your own blood.
Your broken body
and spilt blood have set me
free from the chains of evil.

You see me
with such tenderness
and attentiveness
that not even a hair
can fall from my head
outside of your care.

Every detail
of my body and soul
belongs to you and is held
with constant kindness
in your heart.

There is no hour of my life
that is lived outside your care.

No part of me will ever be lost.

You are presently gathering up
all the shattered pieces of me,
together with all the broken
pieces of this earth
into a brilliant world
that will never die.

Every moment of my story
is but a movement in your hands
to make all things whole.

Because I belong,
your very Spirit lives within me,
companioning me into courage
even when I have none.

Everywhere I go,
there you are.

Because I belong,
I am being made ready
and willing to live my life
as a discovery of your presence,
to become a conduit
of the joy that radiates
from you.

Lord Jesus,
you are my courage,
my comfort, and
my irrevocable crown.

Beginning here, I glimpse the end of fear.
John stands in the river. Christ walks right in.
These are the steps that show how Love draws near.
Heaven is torn open. The Dove descends.

Before the Son has done any great sign,
the Voice who made the world, makes love a gift.
Through cloud and sun, God speaks the true design:
"You are beloved." Love now is in earth's midst.

The river's course remains the same and yet
these words have stirred the world, tilting faith's flow.
Love is not earned, nor won, but heard and set
on he who asked to be baptized below.

This Man still hears the words for which we reach.
Beloved becomes our truth in God's own speech.

Jesus replied, "Foxes have dens and birds have nests, but the Son of Man has no place to lay his head."
MATTHEW 8:20 NIV

Homeless Lord,

Though the Father
crowned you Prince of Peace,
you had no place to lay your head.

Build compassion within us
that we might see your face
in those who do not have a place
to lay their heads and hearts in safety
and that we might trust your peace
can dwell with us
in our own weary
wandering.

You are our eternal home.

Amen.

Jesus, full of the Holy Spirit, returned from the Jordan and was led by the Spirit in the wilderness, where for forty days he was tested by the devil. He ate nothing at all during those days, and when they were over, he was famished.

LUKE 4:1–2 NRSV

Hungry Son,

The Father called you Beloved
and then the Spirit
led you like a lamb
out into the scorching sun

where you
chose trust
in your Father
over proving
your own power.

Lead us to landscapes
we would not choose
to feed us with trust
we cannot lose.

Because for far too long
we've been fed sugar
by shepherds on stages
in words that say fame
and power
and the removal of pain
are the proof
of bearing your name.

But your sonship reveals
what no stage can show:

it is *into* vulnerability
that you choose
to go.

Amen.

Because so many people were coming and going that they did not even have a chance to eat, he said to them, "Come with me by yourselves to a quiet place and get some rest." So they went away by themselves in a boat to a solitary place. But many who saw them leaving recognized them and ran on foot from all the towns and got there ahead of them. When Jesus landed and saw a large crowd, he had compassion on them, because they were like sheep without a shepherd. So he began teaching them many things.

MARK 6:31–34 NIV

I couldn't stop
following
this man.

When he left in a boat
I ran. Like crashing waves
find calm at the shore,
in his face I found
a hope I couldn't ignore.

My stomach is growling.
My feet ache with pain.
But something about him
keeps calling my name.

Most folks I know
are headed away
to the Holy City
to eat and to pray.

But a cloud in my heart
tugs like a kite,
drawing me and a crowd
to this wilderness sight.

And just like my people
once stepped through a sea,
a fire within keeps igniting me

to walk away from the place
I've been taught to find
mercy and might
sitting enshrined.

I've always been hungry.
I've never felt seen.
Most of the teachers
have called me unclean.

But now I'm catching my breath
on the other side of the water
and can't believe what I see.
This man, he is crying,
like his heart has been halved
by the crowd crossing the sea.

Did Mercy
just look
at me?

Show me a shepherd who listens long, who is not afraid of being seen as wrong. Show me a shepherd who will sit on your couch, who asks how you're doing when you've dropped off the earth. Show me a shepherd who cries when you weep, whose heart is still moved by every hurt sheep. Show me a shepherd who gives up their time, who counts not the minutes they're falling behind. Show me a shepherd whose kindness can preach louder than any sermon could reach. Show me a shepherd who studies the language of hearts as much as Hebrew or Greek, who conjugates the verbs of being meek. Show me a shepherd who dares to believe stories whose truths might make people leave. Show me a shepherd who reports abuse, who respects people for more than their use. Show me a shepherd who assumes there's no stage as important as sitting with sheep in their pain.

I LACK

By this time it was late in the day, so his disciples came to him. "This is a remote place," they said, "and it's already very late. Send the people away so that they can go to the surrounding countryside and villages and buy themselves something to eat." But he answered, "You give them something to eat."

MARK 6:35-37 NIV

Jesus,

When your disciples
saw a hungry crowd,
you saw people
starving for love
to reach down.

Teach us to see

lack is only a litmus
test of needing
empathy.

Because you persist
in doing the miracle
of making mercy
a meal.

But to be fed
we all first
must be
seen.

Amen.

Praise
lifts our hands
but lament holds
our hardest prayers.

Holiness
hides nothing
and widens everything.

And you
were made
for a Love
that cannot
be contained.

I shall not want
except that I do.
I want a Shepherd
who comes through.

I want my stress
to be wrapped
in God's arms.
I want my life
to be healed
from all harm.

Perhaps it would
be better to say
I lack nothing
because Love
will stay.

NOTHING

"Truly I tell you, if you have faith as small as a mustard seed, you can say to this mountain, 'Move from here to there,' and it will move. Nothing will be impossible for you."

MATTHEW 17:20 NIV

Jesus,

you who blessed faith
as small as a seed:

reveal the mystery
of faith's abundance
in meekness not might,

that in ourselves
and those we meet
we too would
bless the bravery
of starting off small.

Amen.

As the artist pulls
paint across canvas
until color and light
are wed in joyous sight,

you were a thought
so beautiful in
God's mind

that you
had to
exist.

You are the art
God did not need
and yet wanted so much
that he knelt on the ground
of his new world and painted
the dirt with the brush of his breath until
your heart and lungs and limbs were
birthed from his.

God,

who dreamed up autumn:

grant us imagination
to trust our lives
can grow like trees
that never fear
losing their leaves.

Amen.

"I no longer call you servants, because a servant does not know his master's business. Instead, *I have called you friends*, for everything that I learned from my Father I have made known to you."
JOHN 15:15 NIV, EMPHASIS ADDED

Creator and Sustainer,

who with a word
spoke skies and seas
into being from nothing:

speak life

into the empty space

of my depleted energy

that in your words I might trust:

you are the God
of new beginnings
and I am the friend
whose void
your word
will fill.

Amen.

Jesus directed them to have all the people sit down in
groups on the green grass. So they sat down in groups
of hundreds and fifties.
MARK 6:39–40 NIV

Jesus,

When you spoke
the crowd rested.

Speak now
to we who are
addicted to haste,
for we have lost
the pace of grace.

May we listen.
May we hear.

Rest is a gift
to receive,
not a punishment
to fear.

Amen.

Sometimes rest
is the most
courageous
work of all.

He was in the stern, asleep on the cushion; and they woke him up and said to him, "Teacher, do you not care that we are perishing?" He woke up and rebuked the wind, and said to the sea, "Peace! Be still!" Then the wind ceased, and there was a dead calm.

MARK 4:38-39 NRSV

Jesus, our napping friend,

    When the sea
        churned past all sky,
        drowning daylight in its heft,
            the towering waves beat so hard
        that your friends feared
    they couldn't stay afloat,
and you were asleep
    in the bottom
        of the boat.
            And though we know
        you awoke, though your words
    stilled the waves and lulled
the wind to a whisper,

we still need you to show us
　　　where you are still in our storms.
　　Because like your first friends,
we are drenched through.
　　The waves keep crashing,
　　　and we can't see you.
　　　　You seem to be napping,
　　so it's hard to believe
your lack of concern
isn't a lack of care.
　　But, Christ, every storm
　　　still obeys your voice.
　　　　Amen.

You are a person,
not a performance.

Jesus got them all to sit down in groups of fifty or a hundred—they looked like a patchwork quilt of wildflowers spread out on the green grass! He took the five loaves and two fish, lifted his face to heaven in prayer, blessed, broke, and gave the bread to the disciples, and the disciples in turn gave it to the people. He did the same with the fish. They all ate their fill. The disciples gathered twelve baskets of leftovers. More than five thousand were at the supper.

MARK 6:39–44 MSG

Jesus,

You made sure
the people were sitting
so they could see

the miracle
that follows
the breaking.

May we sit still
in our wilderness
where we can't
see any food.

Because you
always spread
a feast
when you
ask us
to rest.

Amen.

"I myself will gather the remnant of my flock out of all the countries where I have driven them and will bring them back to their pasture, where they will be fruitful and increase in number. I will place shepherds over them who will tend them, and they will no longer be afraid or terrified, nor will any be missing," declares the Lord.

JEREMIAH 23:3–4 NIV

"Because you shove with flank and shoulder, butting all the weak sheep with your horns until you have driven them away, I will save my flock, and they will no longer be plundered. I will judge between one sheep and another. I will place over them one shepherd, my servant David, and he will tend them; he will tend them and be their shepherd."

EZEKIEL 34:21–23 NIV

Jesus, the Promised Shepherd,

you who are always making a way
for your people to rest
when other shepherds demand
performance and success:

reveal the green pastures
where we can heal

that we, the plundered,
may become those
who thunder
kindness as the sound
of a Shepherd's kingdom,
where mercy
abounds.

Amen.

When we see
we have a Good Shepherd,
we don't have to shove
our way to significance.

In Jesus' flock, you do not
have to be shiny to be seen.

He seeks out the struggling,
not the strong. This is a flock
where you do not have to
fight to be found.

Then Jesus, the anger again welling up within him, arrived at the tomb. It was a simple cave in the hillside with a slab of stone laid against it. Jesus said, "Remove the stone."

Then he shouted, "Lazarus, come out!" And he came out, a cadaver, wrapped from head to toe, and with a kerchief over his face. Jesus told them, "Unwrap him and let him loose."

JOHN 11:38, 43-44 MSG

Indignant Christ,

With anger on your lips,
you raised the dead.

Bless now our anger,
anxiety, and anguish

so that these energies
society silences
can break forth with strength
to demand death's violence
be removed like a stone
from the tomb
of our world.

Amen.

You do not need to think
your way to faith,
fierce enough to frighten
fragility into a footnote.

You do not need to lace
your lips with lustrous prayers
or pound your chest in penance
for the puzzle of your pain.

You do not need to be
hopeful or pleasant,
stumbling severed from your story
and the truth your body bears.

You only need to let
your hidden hurt
come with you
and reach your fingers
toward the Love who stands
with scars still on his hands.

Your body brings
your story
everywhere you go.
And faith says
come with me;
I won't leave you
alone.

Come whole,
weary, weak
to the corners
where you've long
been pushed aside.

Come with the courage
of the crucified.

His body brings
his story
everywhere
we go.

And faith says,

he comes with me;
he won't leave me
alone.

Your body brings
your story
where Christ
makes you
his home.

A woman was there who had been subject to bleeding for twelve years, but no one could heal her. She came up behind him and touched the edge of his cloak, and immediately her bleeding stopped.
LUKE 8:43-44 NIV

Jesus,

you who lived so aware
you could sense a woman's dare
to touch the hem of your robe in trust
that in your orbit her suffering
could scatter like dust:

you are the one
who honors those
who risk hoping
to be well.

Help us hear
that you have noticed
we are here

so we can receive
what you promised her,
a life that is healed and whole.

Amen, our Healer and Lord.

Jesus knew that the Father had put him in complete charge of everything, that he came from God and was on his way back to God. So he got up from the supper table, set aside his robe, and put on an apron. Then he poured water into a basin and began to wash the feet of the disciples, drying them with his apron. When he got to Simon Peter, Peter said, "Master, *you* wash *my* feet?"

JOHN 13:3-6 MSG

Lord,

You are the Shepherd
who is always more ready
to serve than we are
to be served.

Wash us with the water
of your welcome.
Wipe our imaginations
clean of the assumption
that we are too dirty to love.

May we let you love us
down to the dirt under our toenails
and the darkness in the crevices of our souls
and so learn the direction of love is down.

For you are the God
who gets on the ground.

If God keeps track of your tears
and holds them safe in a bottle,

then perhaps
your pain is precious.

Perhaps
your tears
tell truth.

Perhaps
you don't have to stop
the flow of what God
wants to hold as a treasure.

—crying is holy.

"Pray this doesn't help," my dad warned through the phone. The night is cold and the fog outside my window has decided to be bold, covering the cliff behind my dorm in a cloud. Orbs of light stand sentinel in the distance, marking the borders of a gray world that was once green.

I turn away from the window and use my palms to close my silver flip phone and nearly drop it to the carpeted ground. My fingers are like swollen, curved sausages. I hear my roommate in the study room next door, rustling through a desk. She emerges with my keys and holds my hands as I stand. Heat rises from my flushed cheeks. I hate this and I need this. She hooks her arm under mine, and we take one tiny step after another until we reach my truck. She is driving me across campus to a friend who has a bathtub in her room. I'm thinking how much I hate how my body seems like a tomb.

I strip and cannot slip into the tub. I call to my friend to help me lift my leaden legs over its white porcelain lip. I am naked and need relief more than respect. Steam rises from the aquamarine water in welcome. My friend sinks onto the cold chipped tiles beside the tub as the water envelops my fingers and toes. She is clearly unashamed of this show.

I weep

because the water is helping.

I weep

because the water is like an X-ray,
and my body is betrayed.

Thirteen years later, and I still sink with pain beyond what I can see or speak. But in the water, it is grace that I seek. Naked, I cannot forsake my need. The quiet water drowns my doubt. I sink into the crystal embrace, and now there is no room left for hate. The water is a symbol. The bath is a sign: I cannot hate my body, for she is me, and she is mine.

Then he took a deep breath and breathed into them.
"Receive the Holy Spirit," he said.
JOHN 20:22 MSG

O God,

In the beginning
there was Breath.
The earth was empty.
The darkness was deep.
And your Wind blew over it all.

Hover over the abyss
of our anxiety today

that our barrenness
might become a beginning
and our breathlessness
but lungs to fill

through Christ our Shepherd
who does not only refresh our souls
but brings them back to life
by the same Spirit who
breathed this world into being
and is blowing
in us still.

Amen.

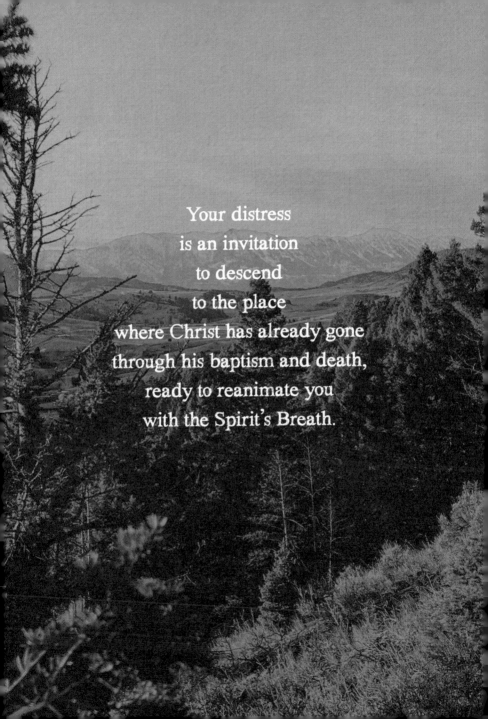

Your distress
is an invitation
to descend
to the place
where Christ has already gone
through his baptism and death,
ready to reanimate you
with the Spirit's Breath.

Trauma pierces us.

But there is nothing
that trauma has severed
that God is not presently
holding together.

There is no part of you
that is beyond Christ's care.

He is patient, and he is present.

Christ is holding us together
by the power of his Spirit,
wrapping scarred hands securely around
the most shattered pieces of our stories,
carrying them with care because

he chose to be shattered first.

The Broken One knows beauty
is not a matter of perfection
but placement. He takes
our shards and situates them
within his story.

He makes us a mosaic of glory.

Your hope doesn't lie
in being strong enough
to not be shattered. Your hope
is that you will always be held
in an Artist's hands.

Trauma can take us there.

Where your past, present, and future
are all held together in the tender hands
of the God who chose to be pierced
so that your past and present
will become a future of peace.

Faith is not mustering up
courage to no longer be broken.

Faith
is practicing
the courage to name
even your broken pieces
as beloved.

Why,
when the world has so wounded us,
do we embrace a new day?

Because
the sky still dances a blush ballet.

Because
though you seem besieged by pain,
your breath remains.

You
carry the cadence of creation
in your two mighty lungs.

So,
call your soul out from her cave.

Ask
her, gently, to be brave.

Let
go of the way you've been telling
the story of these days.

Your
breath remains.

Hope
returns as you realize
your breath was never meant to be held.

It
was given
and in giving it attention,
love lifts you up from pain.

And
so, we bless the day.

"Anyone who intends to come with me has to let me lead. You're not in the driver's seat—I am. Don't run from suffering; embrace it. Follow me and I'll show you how."
LUKE 9:23 MSG

Jesus,

You say words
we hate hearing,

but you never
demanded anything
you were not willing
to live first.

Tune our ears
to recognize the syllables of love
thrumming through the sentences
that make us shudder.

For your resurrection
reminds us
that suffering
can shift us
into a better story.

Amen.

When your dream has withered,
find your way to a river.

Watch the way the water shimmers
when touched by the sun,
how she flows in one direction
around boulders and over rocks.

The water trusts its current
will not be blocked.

And though she may be covered
in ice and in snow,
underneath it all
the water still flows.

Make your place among the boulders
and the cottonwood trees.
It is here that you'll remember
the order of things.

In the desert outside of Tucson, scientists dreamed up an experiment to re-create the conditions of earth for space, when and if the earth could not be made great again. The biosphere was a little world, with its own deserts and rainforests, whose trees grew fast and tall. But one by one, the trees started to fall. And though the biosphere seemed perfect and pure, the scientists forgot one piece of flourishing is air. The little world lacked wind. Without gentle breezes or fierce, strong storms, the trees shot up while the roots stayed small.

And now, facing a thick forest of limber pine and subalpine fir, I smell the resin of resilience. I see the legacy of wind. These trees stand tall because storms have forced their roots to sprawl. They sway in the wind, as to a song. The harder the wind blows, the deeper our roots grow. Resistance is part of resilience. So welcome the wind.

"Here it is again, the Great Reversal: many of the first ending up last, and the last first."

MATTHEW 20:16 MSG

O Good Shepherd,

You led by seeking
the last, the least, and the lost
and succeeded by dying
upon a cross.

Give us the nerve
to name the cost

of confusing righteousness
with affluence and trading
relationship for dominance.

Grant us the faith
to see we are lost;

that we might return
to the right path with you,
the one that is rutted
with relationships
that are kind
and true.

Amen.

Be gentle
toward all
that remains
unhealed in you.

The space
between today's hurt
and tomorrow's healing
is sacred ground.

Each step
you take is but
a footfall on a path
Christ already
walked before you.

Each breath
you take is one
the Spirit breathes in you.

Time and space
are nothing to God and grace.

Be hospitable
toward all that still hurts.

Maybe even
linger.

There is
a friend within
all that is unfinished.

"There's trouble ahead when you live only for the approval of others, saying what flatters them, doing what indulges them. Popularity contests are not truth contests—look how many scoundrel preachers were approved by your ancestors! Your task is to be true, not popular."

LUKE 6:26 MSG

Jesus,

You are
the Way,
the Truth,
and the Life.

Show us the way out
of living for others' approval
and into authenticity;

that we might walk in the confidence
of our unchanging worth to you
and so carry your courage
to speak costly truths,
for it is in the task
to be true to you
that we receive
life that
lasts.

Amen.

Last weekend
I repotted my plants.
Some were scraggly,
some drooping, some
spilling over the edges
of their mismatched pots,
stretching toward
the windows and over
each other for light.

I set out yellow bags of soil
and terra-cotta pots
all across the white kitchen table,
determined to prove
my husband wrong
that I am not, indeed,
a plant killer in disguise.

It was annoying,
the necessary mess,
but it wasn't until I reached in

and the dirt got under
every last fingernail
that I realized:

what we call unruly
and disruptive
is often just a plant
needing a bigger pot.

You are allowed to outgrow
the old pots of communities
and certainties
that once held you
but now hinder you.

You can plant
your life and work
among people who
celebrate your presence.

You do not have to sink your roots
down any farther into soil
that is now taking more nutrients
from you than it gives.

May you have courage
to grow
as large
as your capacity.

May you have curiosity
to expand into your largeness
with trust that God
looks after your limits.

May you have kindness
to bless the space
that held you
up 'til now.

May you have wisdom
to see how cramped pots
holding the soil of scarcity
keep you and others small.

May you have ferocity
to seek places
spacious enough
for your soul
to grow strong.

FOR HIS NAME'S SAKE

Within minutes they were bickering over who of them would end up the greatest. But Jesus intervened: "Kings like to throw their weight around and people in authority like to give themselves fancy titles. It's not going to be that way with you. Let the senior among you become like the junior; let the leader act the part of the servant."
LUKE 22:24–26 MSG

Jesus,

You told your friends
fancy titles are fiction
when it comes to
God's benediction.

Speak again,
for we often tether
your glory to a crown.

We give away our goodness
to those who tear us down.

Let us hear you so we'll know:
your name's sake means
you'll never let us go.

Amen.

There will be no peace in your soul
until you give up seeking
the approval of people
who misuse power
to keep you small.

You are not a brick
in the building
of someone else's fame.

Shalom is in the sound
of the Shepherd's voice
calling you by name.

Follow this lone voice,
even if he leads
far from comfort
and certainty.

The one true Shepherd
of your soul
only uses power
to make you whole.

"I am the good shepherd. The good shepherd lays down his life for the sheep. The hired hand is not the shepherd and does not own the sheep. So when he sees the wolf coming, he abandons the sheep and runs away. Then the wolf attacks the flock and scatters it. The man runs away because he is a hired hand and cares nothing for the sheep."

JOHN 10:11–13 NIV

Jesus, our Good Shepherd,

you who laid down
your life for your sheep:
reaffirm that we
belong in your flock–

that our fear of abandonment
would flee like a thief,
leaving only the assurance
that you will never desert
us, your sheep.

For this we praise:
the glory of your name
can never be fenced off
from our good.

PART

II

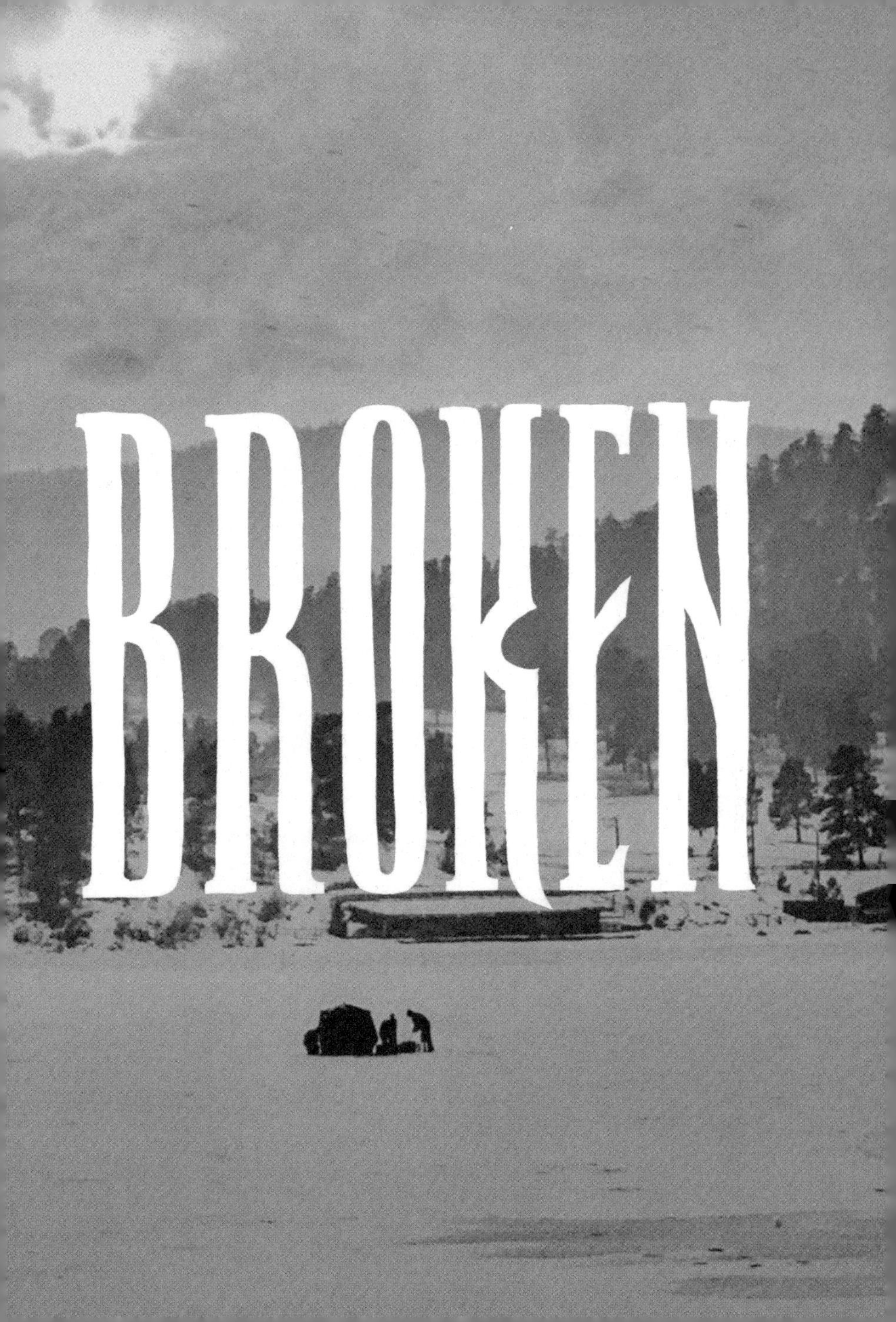
BROKEN

EVEN THOUGH

Jesus said to her, "I am the resurrection and the life. The one who believes in me will live, even though they die; and whoever lives by believing in me will never die. Do you believe this?"
JOHN 11:25-26 NIV

Lord Jesus Christ,

In you is life
that can never die.

Bind your faith
to our doubt
so that even though shadows
sometimes stretch across our trust
and the twilight of life is sure,
darkness will become
a discovery
of your love
and our faith
will rise with you.

Amen.

May you refuse to do battle
against the parts of yourself
that need love the most.

Set down your sword.
Say hello to every shard.

Hello, grief.
Hello, sadness.
Hello, anger.
Hello, madness.

The sharp pieces of you
don't need to be discarded.

The parts that have been hiding
need gentleness and care.

It takes courage to shed off all your armor
in a heap upon the ground,
but there is life inside you
that refuses to go to war.

The story you have shielded.
The self you have disguised.
When you decline the violence
of being someone else,
they will unite in kindness
to build joy into your home.

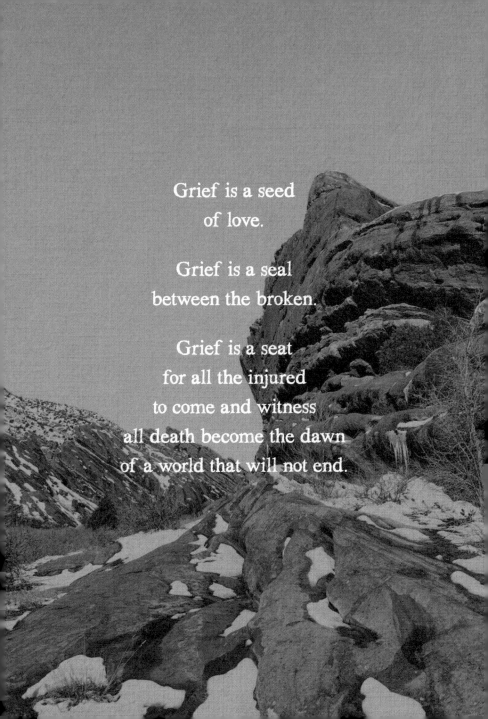

Grief is a seed
of love.

Grief is a seal
between the broken.

Grief is a seat
for all the injured
to come and witness
all death become the dawn
of a world that will not end.

I WALK

God of Moses and Miriam,

who brought your people
through the wilderness:

lead us through the wilderness
of our wounds by the light
of the Wounded One.

For though our anxiety leaves us
lost, alone, and ashamed
and we curse the chaos
in our very selves,

the only way out
of the country
of our wounds
is through,

and Christ's courage
to let chaos
nail him through
can make these wounds the path
back to our promised land.

Amen.

Stress paints only
in black and gray.
It copies the same
picture down
day after day.

Your mind is an artist
of anticipation. She needs
the watercolors of movement
and the brushes of beauty
to expect love to come your way.

When anger clouds over hope
and grief shuts the gate to joy,
there is still a path.

Let your faith have feet.
Let your lungs expand with air.

The cloud-flecked sky can tell
a more spacious story than stress,
and your feet can walk a prayer.

O Lord, our Rock and Refuge,

Our desire for integrity
has outweighed our wish
to protect ourselves
from being wounded.

God, remind us
of the blessing
that only the broken
can hear.

Show us that the storms
raging within us
are but small shadows
of the storm of your fury
to fight for our justice
and vindication.

Confirm that in leaving
people and places,
we have not left
your blessing behind.
It follows us like the rain
of tears down our cheeks.

Lift our eyes to the cross,
where Jesus' broken body
still speaks through groans
that it is among the broken
that your blessing resides.

For you are
not only our Rock.

You are our Rescue.

THROUGH

Jesus,

You left your disciples
instructions for failing.

You gave them grace in advance
for the days they'd be judged
as far from worthy
of listening and love.

Move our feet
from quaking to shaking,
delighted in the dance of recognition,
that no matter who rejects us or you,

we remain friends
that you see through.

Amen.

We would rather be shattered than silenced.
We would rather be disturbed than dismissive.
We would rather be heartbroken than hollow.
We would rather be vulnerable than vacuous.
We would rather be burdened than bullies.
We would rather be maligned than mean.
We would rather be aching than arrogant.
We would rather be vilified than vain.
We would rather be crushed than cruel.
God, bind up all the broken pieces of me and your church.
We would rather be in your hands than never at home.
We would rather hurt now than never heal.

*

The sky is a choir of peach and periwinkle.
Tangerine sings soprano.
Each color, a promise.
The spectrum, a story.
The only power fierce enough
to sing your fear to sleep
is beauty.

Only beauty
can sing stronger
than your sense
of scarcity.

Only beauty
can bind you
back together
when bullies seem
to break everything.

Only beauty can
bring you back
to believing God
will give goodness
tomorrow.

Let wonder
wrap herself
around your angst.

You have permission
to find one good gift
for which to give thanks.

Even when the night
needs attention too
—the bills, the invasion,
the diagnoses that loom—
you are allowed to look
for goodness like a clue.

There are gifts
that are hidden
even in gloom:
dust glints like gold
and skies turn sapphire.
Beauty is the oxygen
that feeds the soul's fire.

So when the day is ending
heavy with lack, look up
and let hope
come back.

Fear will keep belting
out an endless loop of pain.
But beauty will sing you
back home again.

"Your eye is a lamp, lighting up your whole body. If you live wide-eyed in wonder and belief, your body fills up with light. If you live squinty-eyed in greed and distrust, your body is a musty cellar. Keep your eyes open, your lamp burning, so you don't get musty and murky. Keep your life as well-lighted as your best-lighted room."

LUKE 11:34–36 MSG

Light of the World,

You said wonder
will fill us with light.

May we look up
to watch for the wonder
that is already here.

Though some say
to keep heaven in mind,

the way to heaven
is straight through our eyes.

Amen.

Jesus went with them to a garden called Gethsemane and told his disciples, "Stay here while I go over there and pray." Taking along Peter and the two sons of Zebedee, he plunged into an agonizing sorrow. Then he said, "This sorrow is crushing my life out. Stay here and keep vigil with me."

MATTHEW 26:36-38 MSG

Our Crushed and Courageous Lord,

you who asked your friends
to stay with you in sorrow:

illuminate the courage
it takes to ask for help
on our dark nights

that we would respect
even our neediness
as an expression
of union with you

and find that we can be both
crushed and courageous too.

Amen.

Blessed are you who have suffered
for within your soul are storehouses
of the stories you have survived.

When darkness shadows the harvest
of your hardest years,
you can still dip deep
into the grain of your grief
and plumb the well of your tears.

Taste the truth of your persistence.
Swallow the strength that brought you here.
Digest the discouragement of today.
And then   hope will appear.

You are more than the stories
that have shaped you.
But because of them,
you   grew.

Inside your soul is a silo.
You've always held
more strength
than you knew.

A sudden fog
fell on our future.
More than faith,
we feel frightened.
More than fear,
we feel lost.

We lift up our eyes,
but we only see clouds.
Our bodies brace
for what may fall.
Nothing seems certain.
Fear lurks, tall.

Lord, these clouds conceal
your face, our faith.

When grace seems hidden
behind thick clouds,
give us the courage
to trust they are filled
with needed rain.

Guide us
into the cloud
of our unknowing.

Spirit, stir us
to greet our grief
with compassion.

Christ, make us
willing to witness
our world as it is.

Father, help us
hear your voice
guiding us through the fog.

And, Lord, we pray:
may this disorientation
be a door.

When we feel lost,
may we risk
being found.

Amen.

When you were stuck in your old sin-dead life, you were incapable of responding to God. God brought you alive—right along with Christ! Think of it! All sins forgiven, the slate wiped clean, that old arrest warrant canceled and nailed to Christ's cross. He stripped all the spiritual tyrants in the universe of their sham authority at the Cross and marched them naked through the streets.

COLOSSIANS 2:13-15 MSG

Lord,

I fear I am both
too far from faithful
and too close to frustrating.

But the only measurement
that matters is the distance
between your two nail-scarred hands
that closed the chasm
between my fear
and your friendship
forever.

Mark me by scars
that I would measure
my worth by your courage.

Amen.

Religion said sanctification
meant making myself small.

The church handed me scissors
and commanded, Get to work.
Cut away all the parts of you
that are "flesh."

I became
more scissors
than a self.

I swallowed
a story of war
as grace.

I made
my mind a general,
barking orders
to march hard.

I declared
corporeal war
for spiritual gain.

Truth against tissue.
Faith against fear.
Holiness against the heart.

I named
my skin an enemy
to subjugate, my feelings
foes to fight, and my desires
rivals to oppose.

I marched
          until
                    I collapsed.

What good
is a Christian soldier
marching as to war
with the cross of Jesus
crushing them into the floor?

My body was never
territory to colonize.

But down on the ground,
in the dirt and the grime,
I could see past the lies
to a riven side.

Holes in hands
spoke peace to mine.

The scissors were never
spiritual. The war was never
divine. The truth was that
this body was already a place
with holiness inside.

Sanctification is like stitching
the sinew to the soul.
And grace is but a thread
sewing mind and body
whole.

The body is not a barrier
between the Bible and belief.
It is the tissue where tenderness
can speak the truth in relief:

your body
is already
the beloved
dwelling place
of God.

This is what the Sovereign Lord, the Holy One of Israel, says:

"In repentance and rest is your salvation,
in quietness and trust is your strength,
but you would have none of it."

ISAIAH 30:15 NIV

"I will strengthen them in the Lord
and in his name they will live securely,"
declares the Lord.

ZECHARIAH 10:12 NIV

Transforming Presence,

Like fire melts iron
and carbon into steel,
you promised to strengthen
and secure those who turn and rest.

Gather now the weight of our stress,
heated in the warmth of the wound in your chest,
that the iron and carbon of every grief and groan
would melt into the strong joy of being known.

You are the Living Alchemist.

"Father, if you are willing, take this cup from me; yet not my will, but yours be done." An angel from heaven appeared to him and strengthened him. And being in anguish, he prayed more earnestly, and his sweat was like drops of blood falling to the ground.

LUKE 22:42-44 NIV

O God who cried for relief in the garden,

Your tears have shown me
that faithfulness does not
mean fearlessness.

Help me see my fear
as the seedbed of faith.

Uncurl my fingers
to sow my anxieties
in the soil of your trustworthiness.

Remind me that this dirt
where I kneel to tend
to both my ordinary needs
and my extraordinary hopes
for myself and for the world
is a place you kneeled before me.

Help me plant peace
where others sow suspicion.

Grow my love for wholeness
to be fiercer than my fear of evil.

Open my eyes this day
to see both the news
and my needs
as sacred ground.

Together, we will plant gardens.

Amen.

Can you stomach a Savior
who felt fear and stress
so acutely that sweat spilled
like drops of blood
from his skin?

Does your theology include
an incarnate God,
whose anxiety was
so great it ruptured
his blood vessels?

If we cannot trace God
in the most human fear,
we won't get to see
him drawing near.

I will not allow myself
to be less human than Christ.

If we cannot be human,
we cannot be upheld.

"I'm speaking to you as dear friends. Don't be bluffed into silence or insincerity by the threats of religious bullies. True, they can kill you, but *then* what can they do? There's nothing they can do to your soul, your core being. Save your fear for God, who holds your entire life—body and soul—in his hands."

LUKE 12:4–5 MSG

Living God and Sustaining Savior,

Religion could not reduce you.
Death could not defeat you.

Receive now our fear.

For in your hands
fear is not final.

Bound to your life
fear burns as
courage's fuel.

Kept in your heart,
we can be courageous,
trusting the core of us
can never be lost.

Amen.

NO EVIL

"Do not be afraid of those who kill the body but cannot kill the soul. Rather, be afraid of the One who can destroy both soul and body in hell. Are not two sparrows sold for a penny? Yet not one of them will fall to the ground outside your Father's care. And even the very hairs of your head are all numbered. So don't be afraid; you are worth more than many sparrows."

MATTHEW 10:28–31 NIV

Jesus,

You say the Father cares,
but the sparrow still falls.

Grant us
the courage
to suffer.

Because in this story,
we only fall
into your hands.

To the praise of the One
who holds all things together.

"I'm not okay"
is sacred speech.

"Help!"
is a full prayer.

Trauma steals our tongues,
so it's surprising the main way
many pastors approach hurt
is to preach away pain.

When harm happens,
the senselessness of hate
temporarily severs
the body from the brain.

Like a screw gone missing,
we're unfastened from the hinge
that opens the door
to make sense
of our experience.

We cannot name and tame
the truth of our wounds
until we are held
safe through our fears.

Courage starts
with consenting
to be present.

What if your struggles
don't need sermons to relent?
There are other ways
to shepherd your soul.
Your pain can be a place
to be soothed back to being whole.

Trauma steals our tongues
but courage is embodied.

Shepherds like Christ
bear witness to pain.

Trauma happens and harms us.
But I often wonder
if the worst trauma
is the second wave—
when your story is misbelieved,
mistrusted, and maligned.

May your story
find safe harbor
in the presence of people
who will honor both
your vulnerability
and resilience.

While he lived on earth, anticipating death, Jesus cried out in pain and wept in sorrow as he offered up priestly prayers to God. Because he honored God, God answered him. Though he was God's Son, he learned trusting-obedience by what he suffered, just as we do. **HEBREWS 5:7-8** MSG

O Jesus,

the God whose eyes cried tears
and whose hands hold
all things together:

we, the weary, ask
that where we see chaos and want certainty,
you'd give calmness and forge courage

that we might walk
into this new week and season
welcoming you as both Companion and Creator
in a world being entirely made new.

Amen.

This is the day our eyes
sharpen to see
a realm where might
comes in meekness
and wholeness
arrives in weakness.

This is the day our hearts
soften to hold
a hope that comes down lower
than in religion we were told.

Omnipotent God
became a baby
at a breast.

Omniscient God,
who would die
after begging
for rest.

You cannot descend lower
than he chose to go.
You are never weaker
than he welcomes.
You are never more forsaken
than he felt.

This is the God of the killed,
the conquered,
the sick, and
the bound.

Ours is the God
who came down
to the ground.

He stoops lower
than we want to go
and down in the dirt
he breathes us into being
never alone.

Your tender heart

is not a liability

or immaturity.

Your tender heart

is a holy place

where God

shows you

his face.

Sometimes when I am sitting in centering prayer, my hands wrap around a mug of black coffee and my eyes find my dogs lying down beside me in a puddle of light. And I smile, just delighted that they exist. And I smile, just delighted to realize again my joy in them is simply one infinitesimal fraction of God's delight in being with me. Take the thing that stretches a smile across your face and multiply it by a million. You will be nowhere close to how glad God is to be with you.

Now may the God of peace, who through the blood of
the eternal covenant brought back from the dead our
Lord Jesus, that great Shepherd of the sheep, equip
you with everything good for doing his will, and may he
work in us what is pleasing to him, through Jesus Christ,
to whom be glory for ever and ever. Amen.

HEBREWS 13:20–21 NIV

Jesus,

you who are
the great Shepherd
of the sheep:

Lay your staff
across our shoulders
to remind us you are near.

Invert our expectation
of equipping and care,
that you'll mostly shepherd us
by scolding or somehow punish
us into love.

For your staff is not
a rod of correction
but the extension of your voice
to reassure us there is no place
we can go that is outside
of your scope.

Amen.

David could sing of God's comfort
because he had learned to trust
the pounding of fear
is not the absence of love.

When he sang of God's rod
and staff as his consolation,
he had to remember
the days he was delivered.

Out in the fields, far from home
and far from help, the shepherd
boy was tutored in the language
of care. He loved his sheep
like family. He watched closely
for snares. Evening and morning,
their security was his prayer.

He practiced for the worst,
when bigger animals would try
to make his precious sheep
into their evening meal. He
threw his rod at the trees
until it became an art. He
was ready for the day. He
was ready for the night.

One day, with a crack on a branch,
he spun and saw
a bear on the ridge
—a sheep in his mouth.

And with one breath,
David's fear turned to strength.
He threw his rod without thinking.
He saved his sheep from the threat.

David knew it in his bones
more than he knew it in his head:

courage is the art
of protecting what we love.

One night he had to write
of the joy that fixed the stars,
of the Lord who is his Shepherd,
who day after night, taught him
to love his sheep without lack
more than he feared
losing his life.

They stripped him and put a scarlet robe on him, and then twisted together a crown of thorns and set it on his head. They put a staff in his right hand. Then they knelt in front of him and mocked him. "Hail, king of the Jews!" they said. They spit on him, and took the staff and struck him on the head again and again. After they had mocked him, they took off the robe and put his own clothes on him. Then they led him away to crucify him.

MATTHEW 27:28-31 NIV

Son of David, Son of God,

Just like David, at whose rod
and staff Goliath jeered,
the powers of empire
chose to mock you.

Meet us in our mocking,
where power laughs
at our demise,
for their taunting
can't tell
the full truth
of how we'll rise.

In the quiet power
of the Spirit,
we say yes
and amen.

My God, my God, why have you forsaken me?
  Why are you so far from saving me,
    so far from my cries of anguish?
PSALM 22:1 NIV

About three in the afternoon Jesus cried out in a loud
voice, *"Eli, Eli, lema sabachthani?"* (which means "My
God, my God, why have you forsaken me?").
MATTHEW 27:46 NIV

Forsaken One,

David's hard words
stretched out of your lips
like a staff gathering up the past
into your present.

And now we ask that your cry
would echo in our prayers,
hooking us gently
where we are ensnared

that in our worst fears
we would come to fathom:
honesty about our hopelessness
precedes resurrection.

Amen.

Prayer
is not
constant
positivity.

It is honesty
held in our hands
and hurled at the sky.

When David dared
to curse at the air
and Christ cried
from the cross
that the Father
was not there,
they both
pierced
a hole

in the
universe's clouds,
and now Love's ears
are tuned to the sound
of candor and cries
as much as praise
rings out.

The world has forever
been widened
for worship.

Our worst words
of self-pity and
loudest wails
now have become
welcomed prayers.

Christ's prayer
pierced
the veil.

Thomas, sometimes called the Twin, one of the Twelve, was not with them when Jesus came. The other disciples told him, "We saw the Master."

But he said, "Unless I see the nail holes in his hands, put my finger in the nail holes, and stick my hand in his side, I won't believe it."

Eight days later, his disciples were again in the room. This time Thomas was with them. Jesus came through the locked doors, stood among them, and said, "Peace to you."

Then he focused his attention on Thomas. "Take your finger and examine my hands. Take your hand and stick it in my side. Don't be unbelieving. Believe."

Thomas said, "My Master! My God!"

JOHN 20:24-28 MSG

Friend of Doubters,

When Thomas the twin
was shocked
by the course of your story,
you held out your hands
and let your scars speak
him back to belief.

Comfort us in our doubt,
shock, and fear with the solace
only scars can bring.

Because though
we cannot see you,
like Thomas, we reach.
And though we cannot touch
the wound in your side,
the mystery of faith is double—
that somehow in our wounds
you reside, and doubters
become the first
to call you Divine.

Amen.

If being in church hurts,
if the gathering of saints
brings grief instead of gratitude,

rise gently in your soul to safety.
Don't be afraid to step outside.

Sit down on a bench, far
from praise and others' ploys.
Give your body a chance
to feel the relief
of not having to guard yourself
from watching eyes.
Remember how to breathe
as the sun warms you
in her gaze.

On the margins, you
are not outside grace.

If the Body feels like a pile
of deconstructed beams
and upturned nails,
a faith without a home
or a people to call your own,
look at the One
who cried in anguish
in a garden alone.

On the margins, you
are never outside his love.

If the communion of saints
crushed you, remember:
others crushed him first
and the breaking
bought our lives.

On the margins, Christ
takes rubble and discarded joists
in his scarred and tender hands
and makes us
the restored foundation
of a church where love
joins every part.

On the margins, we
are not outside his hands,
his love, his grace, his heart.

Christ fell
while carrying
his cross
and was
still faithful.

Be encouraged.
You can still
be faithful
while falling
when carrying
yours.

PART

III

Jesus said, "Make the people sit down." There was a nice carpet of green grass in this place. They sat down, about five thousand of them. Then Jesus took the bread and, having given thanks, gave it to those who were seated. He did the same with the fish. All ate as much as they wanted.

JOHN 6:10–11 MSG

Unconventional Lord,

The first miracle
of feeding the crowds
was that you chose
to slow down.

The second, we miss, but
is staggering just the same:
in preparing a meal,
like a woman you became.

It was from both
inclusion and generosity
that a whole crowd ate.

Kindle by your Spirit
a fire of new welcome,
humility, and faith in us today
that the yeast of radical belonging
would rise in our midst, driving
all shame and subjugation away.

To the praise of your name,
the Shepherd who saves.

Amen.

have courage
to be a beginner.
entrust your time
to telling a tale
in which the ending is veiled.

build patience
for the harsh voice inside;
she is still a child who believes
perfection is the prerequisite
to belonging.

over and over
I find that behind
every voice of fear in my head
is a child who needs a friend.

introduce yourself.
summon your kindest smile.
ask her what she wished
she was able to do.
and then remind her
you aren't going anywhere.

a beginning
is a beckoning,
an invitation to open
toward the goodness
being prepared deep inside.

to begin
is to befriend.

Now the tax collectors and sinners were all gathering around to hear Jesus. But the Pharisees and the teachers of the law muttered, "This man welcomes sinners and eats with them."
LUKE 15:1-2 NIV

Christ of the table,

you who ate
with the hated
and befriended
those whom others
slighted and silenced:

may we so welcome
the hated parts
of our own selves

because at your table
everyone has a seat
and every story
is worthy
of being
heard.

Amen.

"Or imagine a woman who has ten coins and loses one. Won't she light a lamp and scour the house, looking in every nook and cranny until she finds it? And when she finds it you can be sure she'll call her friends and neighbors: 'Celebrate with me! I found my lost coin!' Count on it—that's the kind of party God's angels throw every time one lost soul turns to God."

LUKE 15:8–10 MSG

Storyteller,

You redefined
what it means
to be lost.

Upend
our expectations
of repentance.

Subvert
our assumptions
of who is lost
and who is found.

Because like
the woman's coin,
we can be lost
right inside
God's house.

But we cherish
that you tell the story
that we are worth
being found.

For this we praise:
the stories you tell
end with joy.

Paradox
is the only table
strong enough
to hold truth.
You can be
weak. You can
be wise. You can
be hurt. You can

still rise

from the table
of truth, fed by food
prepared with tender care.

God combines bitter
herbs with bright spices
to nourish us
not with what we wanted
but what we most need.

Take and eat.
It is only from this table,
fed by these careful hands,
that you will rise strong enough
to endure the tension
of grace.

Almighty and Everlasting God,

You made the world
in a whirl of wind

and by your word
emptiness   became extravagance.

Hover again over the blank spaces
between   our breaths

where the pain of being a person
punches   our chests;

that we might sense
this void   is blessed;

that we might welcome
the wind   is still

where you will make
all things   new.

Amen.

Jesus told them this parable: "Suppose one of you has a hundred sheep and loses one of them. Doesn't he leave the ninety-nine in the open country and go after the lost sheep until he finds it? And when he finds it, he joyfully puts it on his shoulders and goes home. Then he calls his friends and neighbors together and says, 'Rejoice with me; I have found my lost sheep.'"

LUKE 15:3-6 NIV

Jesus, our Shepherd,

You do not blame us
for getting lost.

You search for us
at great personal cost.

Situate us in the story
where we can find
your courage to leave the flock
to bring back the one
who most needs our time;

that we would become
the community of those
who trust we are beloved
enough to risk bringing
the most lost back home.

Amen.

Lost sheep can't make it
home on their own.
They tend to get stuck
between bushes and rocks.

At first they cry
and bleat for help.
But then they grow still
and get quiet to hide
from those who could kill.

But when they hear
the faintest sound
of their Shepherd's
whistle or voice,
they quiver and summon
the strength to cry once more.

Your cries are not
a source of shame to God.

They are the beautiful sound
of your soul being found.

God leaves behind
the ninety-nine
pretty, pleasant parts of you
to find the one part of you
that feels the most unlovable.

There is no part of you
that the Good Shepherd
will not seek and follow
to extend goodness and love.

There is no part of you
that is too broken, too angry,
too irritable, too anxious,
or too lost for God to seek.

The Shepherd searches
over ridges and rocks.
He calls out your name,
though his voice begins to crack.
There is no looming storm
or heavy rain that can call off
his search. He wipes sweat
from his brow and keeps
stepping through the dirt.
His breath has gone stale.
His stomach growls
from missed meals.
But the Shepherd is resolved.
He will not stop.

God's goodness and love hunt
you harder than a lion or a bear.
They follow and track you
longer and farther
than any harm.
This Shepherd is relentless
to recover the parts of you
that are lost. He will not leave
behind the beauty
that others have cursed.

And when he finally finds
the most shamed
parts of you, he stoops
down to the ground
and, through briar and branch,
hooks his staff around your neck
and gently pulls you back.

No matter how muddy
or dirty your wool, he wraps
his hands around your waist
and lifts you across his shoulders.
He knows you're too weak
to make it home on your feet.
But he doesn't mind.
You're his sheep.

What he loved, was lost.
But what was lost, he found.

The wounds that took you
out to the wilderness
are simply the mark
of your worth to him.

To God our Good Shepherd,
there is no larger joy
than bringing you home.

Count on it.

More than anything
you will ever do for God,
God delights in finding
every lost part
of who you are.

Count on it.

When a Samaritan woman came to draw water, Jesus said to her, "Will you give me a drink?" (His disciples had gone into the town to buy food.) The Samaritan woman said to him, "You are a Jew and I am a Samaritan woman. How can you ask me for a drink?" (For Jews do not associate with Samaritans.)

JOHN 4:7–9 NIV

The teachers of the law and the Pharisees brought in a woman caught in adultery. They made her stand before the group and said to Jesus, "Teacher, this woman was caught in the act of adultery. In the Law Moses commanded us to stone such women. Now what do you say?" . . .

But Jesus bent down and started to write on the ground with his finger. When they kept on questioning him, he straightened up and said to them, "Let any one of you who is without sin be the first to throw a stone at her."

JOHN 8:3–5, 6–7 NIV

God of the Hated,

you who sought out
the scorned and the pained:

bless the parts of us
that others have blamed
as too blinded, brash,
and untamed;

because your two hands
of Goodness and Love
ever and always reach
toward the shamed.

Amen.

A shepherd cursed me,
and church became
a source of trauma,
a reminder of pain.

Before I left the church
of my wounds, I stood
at the altar to serve holy food.

The last person to descend
the aisle was the man
who made my life hell.
My heart was pounding
in my chest. And with
one deep breath,
I was given a choice.
I could extend
mercy to him.

The body of Christ
broken for me
was broken
for him too.

The blood of Christ
spilled for me
could cover
this pain too.

In that moment
we were balanced
at the foot of the cross.

It is still
the strange place
where curse meets blessing.

The Eucharist
didn't rescue me
from the trauma
of being condemned
by a man called to bless.

Communion
did not save me
from loss and lament.

But it did give me
a sanctuary
I could carry
out the door.

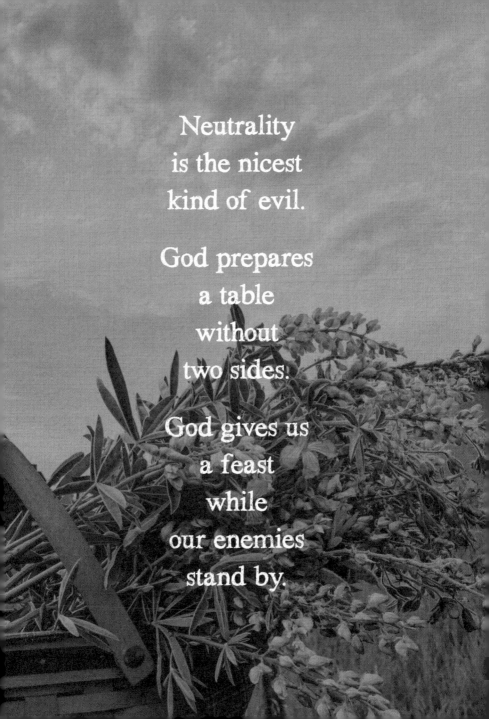

Neutrality
is the nicest
kind of evil.

God prepares
a table
without
two sides.

God gives us
a feast
while
our enemies
stand by.

Almighty God,

Even the darkness
is not dark to you.

Blow on the ember
of faith in our hearts,
for we are in need
of the oxygen of trust

that all the harm
that is done in the dark
will one day become
mere ash and dust.

Consume it all in the fire
of a belonging that is better
than controlling one another.

This we pray
through your Son,
Jesus Christ, who
was betrayed
by a friend
in the night
and put to death
by a government
in plain sight,
yet raised by the Spirit
into indestructible life.

And there he now sits
and reigns with you,
Three-in-One: Father,
Spirit, and Son, all
declaring to darkness:

the light has won.

"But what about you?" he asked. "Who do you say I am?"

Simon Peter answered, "You are the Messiah, the Son of the living God."

Jesus replied, "Blessed are you, Simon son of Jonah, for this was not revealed to you by flesh and blood, but by my Father in heaven. And I tell you that you are Peter, and on this rock I will build my church, and the gates of Hades will not overcome it."

MATTHEW 16:15–18 NIV

Jesus, our Messiah,
the Son of the Living God,

you who gave Simon
a better name
than the shame
that was coming
in denying knowing you
as he stood in the dark,
warming himself
by the flames:

tell us who we are.

Anoint us with a name
we can't disown
on our worst nights.

Because when we are
called by your Voice,
we are confirmed
in a love so strong
no trauma or shame
can revoke
that we belong
in your communion
of saints, the church
whose gates even
hell cannot break.

Amen.

When the Sabbath was over, Mary Magdalene, Mary the mother of James, and Salome bought spices so that they might go to anoint Jesus' body. Very early on the first day of the week, just after sunrise, they were on their way to the tomb and they asked each other, "Who will roll the stone away from the entrance of the tomb?"

But when they looked up, they saw that the stone, which was very large, had been rolled away. As they entered the tomb, they saw a young man dressed in a white robe sitting on the right side, and they were alarmed.

"Don't be alarmed," he said. "You are looking for Jesus the Nazarene, who was crucified. He has risen! He is not here. See the place where they laid him."

MARK 16:1-6 NIV

Son of God
and Son of a Woman,

Women were the ones
who were faithful
to follow you beyond
your final breath.

Bless the brave ones
who follow you,
whom others forget
and fail to honor.

Because like these women,
those who are faithful
to witness death
become the first
to witness resurrection.

Amen.

There are no ashes on my head.

I wanted to make my way down a creaky aisle today.
I wanted to hear my priest speak the truth
that I am dust and to dust I will return.
I wanted liturgy to cut like a knife
through the strands of this season
that seems hell-bent on strapping
me to sickness.

But I spent the entire day in bed.

Forehead bare. Schedule canceled
yet again. Soul-weary of new diagnoses
and scary symptoms and the endlessness of it all.

I know I'm not alone in feeling
like I've been living
an endless Lent.

Today, just as I was lamenting–languishing really–
a knock came to the door. A care package.
A blanket. Orange sunglasses. And the kindest note.

And wrapped in that love on a bench in the cold,
watching the afternoon turn to night, I know:
just like the fire that burned last year's palms into today's ashes,
the purging fire of today is being tended by others with care.

There are no ashes on my head.

There is only hope, burning like a fire
through my hardest days, lighting up incandescent moments
when time folds in on itself and I suddenly see:
human and heavenly hands are tending this blaze
into that which will enrich the brightest blooms.

This fire isn't for nothing.

And long after this fire loses oxygen,
the ash that will remain
will become a source of life.

Not one speck of this soot will be wasted.

All our ash
will nurture
new life.

—Ash Wednesday, 2022

"Father, if you are willing, please take this cup of suffering away from me. Yet I want your will to be done, not mine."
LUKE 22:42 NLT

"I will make them and the places surrounding my hill a blessing. I will send down showers in season; there will be showers of blessing."
EZEKIEL 34:26 NIV

Lord Jesus,

You pulled up a chair
to the table of this earth
and drank the whole cup
of human suffering and hurt.

We ask you to fill
the cups of our lives
to overflow with you.

Make us chalices of your compassion.

Where the world overflows with hatred,
let us hold hope.
Where there is sorrow,
let us savor the sacredness
of every tear-stained face.
Where there is doubt,
let us spill over with grace.

For it is in emptying the cup
of our prejudice that we become filled;
it is in swallowing the wine of sorrow
that we are surprised by grace;
it is in drinking the dregs of doubt
that we digest a love stronger than fear.

Because you held this cup first.

Amen.

A Poem from My Grandma, Jan Bass

I searched and searched
And could not find
A single place for rest
Until the hand of Jesus
Drew me close unto his breast.

He said, My little child,
I see in you no blame.
You are of my choosing.
You're the very reason I came.

I said, My Father God,
What with me would you then do?

And he said, Child, child of mine,
I want only to love you.

If there was only you
And I knew of no other,
Still I would come,
That I could be your brother.

"You must begin with your own life-giving lives. It's who you are, not what you say and do, that counts. Your true being brims over into true words and deeds."
LUKE 6:45 MSG

"Peace I leave with you; my peace I give you. I do not give to you as the world gives. Do not let your hearts be troubled and do not be afraid."
JOHN 14:27 NIV

Living Water,

Your true being
brimmed over
at a table full
of fear. You
poured out
peace. You
spilled out
care.

Tip your love
into our lives
and so make us
people who pour
love where there is pain
and kindness where
there is fear.

May we be filled
so full of your grace
that when we are bumped,
Love will trickle down.

We thank you,
our Generous Friend.

> "Very truly I tell you, unless a kernel of wheat falls to
> the ground and dies, it remains only a single seed. But
> if it dies, it produces many seeds."
> **JOHN 12:24** NIV

Savior,

You are the seed who fell.
Your death broke through the grave.
Your story splits through our wishes
of what it looks like to be brave.

Break open the husk of yesterday's fear.
Bring us words to sever the hard shells
we have grown around our pain

so that the parts
of our stories and selves
that we hate
will become the crevices
where your love
proliferates.

Amen.

Blessed are the broken,
those shattered in spirit by those
who should have made them strong.

Blessed are the grieved
in a world that pretends
positivity will take away pain.

For while the kingdoms
of the able and affluent
corral and crush,

the kingdom of God
is a seed
split open.

May you know
your breaking
is a broadening.

May you trust
your ache
is an awakening.

The kingdom of God
is a seed split open,
and the kingdom
belongs to you.

The one who testifies to these things says, "Surely I am coming soon."

Amen. Come, Lord Jesus!

REVELATION 22:20 NRSV

Grant us, O God, the faith to pray:

Come, Lord Jesus. Help us this day.

For yours is the glory, the honor, the might,
but ours is the sorrow of this long, hard night.

Feed us from your table. Fill us from your wounds.

That your faithful suffering would empower us to trust
that on this day we are not forgotten or condemned but
only being further thrust into the story of a redemption that
nothing can rust, of the kindest Parent, who is coming back soon.

Amen.

One night we sat around an oak table with couples who have lived longer than us. Our plates were piled with pork and polenta, and long after the food was gone, the stories still flowed. They spoke of the times they didn't know how enough money would come. They spoke of the callings that startled their souls.

And in their wrinkled faces, I recognized the outline of my grief. I witnessed my twin longing to see God provide.

And the sheer fact of their existence, of couples who shepherd outside the church's walls, who open doors of belonging that many keep closed, who own houses, and who after all their hard years still look at each other with smiles and tell dad jokes and sputter with more laughter than lament—surely, their bodies did speak a strong sermon to me.

Maybe my story
is still being told.

Maybe we're all just walking each other home to turn the knob of a door to a God who's glad to see us and has prepared for us a place.

Maybe you are not
an exception to grace.

YOUR GOODNESS AND LOVE

Through the heartfelt mercies of our God, God's Sunrise will break in upon us, shining on those in the darkness, those sitting in the shadow of death, then showing us the way, one foot at a time, down the path of peace.

LUKE 1:78–79 MSG

O God, who makes the sun to rise,

Open our eyes to your goodness and love
stretching across the skies,

for we have been hounded
by hatred and lies,

but your beauty
follows us
further
still.

Amen.

We can so easily become
that which has harmed us.

We pour thick concrete
around the softness of our souls
to protect ourselves
from more pain.

Poetry can penetrate
our layers of self-protection.
Beauty can call us
into resurrection.
Like words on the edge
of a cliff into death,
Goodness and Love can pull
us back from the ledge.

A forest can speak hope
in the scent of pine.
A wave can roll grace
to mist our parched pain.
A peony can bloom faith
with ballet skirts
of intricate praise.

Goodness and Love
always do seek
us in the layers,
lodged under hard sheets
of concrete, too thick
to breathe, too precious
to leave. They chase us
all our days and crack
open our shields,
calling us back
home to the beauty
of being healed.

Right now snow covers the soil
on the ridge where red rocks
jut from the foothills, where
I have walked and wept
and wondered at the way

winter is harsh
and spring is muddy.

The ground is barren now,
but in just months she'll sprout.
Come summer, this soil will burst
    with green.
The trail will put on her lavender
    scarf.
The wind will ruffle through
    each bloom.

May today be the day you realize
that if God dreamed wildflowers
into existence from the dirt,
    which rise
season after season from snow-
    covered soil,
through mud and muck and
    storms, then
your blossoms can return from
    winter too.

And if most wildflowers stretch
as rainbows on remote hillsides,
far from trails with human eyes,

your beauty can also be stunning
even if unseen by others' eyes.

Honor the hard ground
where seeds hide under snow.

No farm lives in perpetual
    harvest.
No wildflower blooms all year.

Hallow your hidden work,
how you push through the dirt
year after year, day after day,
choosing kindness over criticism,
forgiveness over fury,
and trust in the truth
that beauty will
eventually
bloom.

You are a perennial.
Your flowers always return.

There is beauty
both in your blooming
and your becoming.

Be tender
toward the time
between both.

If God imagined that small,
    brown seeds
far beneath thick, white snow
could one day curl into damp,
    dark dirt
and spring into whorls of green
with strong, maroon stalks
    crowned
with bell after lavender bell,

then he will curl you in his care,
he will spring your life into
    the air,
he will build bells from your
    small buds,
he will delight in watching who
    you will become,
for you are the flower of
    God's love.

Love is patient.
Love is kind.
Love is   mine.

WILL FOLLOW ME

Lᴏʀᴅ my God, I take refuge in you;
      save and deliver me from all who pursue me.
PSALM 7:1 ɴɪᴠ

But the Pharisees went out and plotted how they might
kill Jesus.
MATTHEW 12:14 ɴɪᴠ

Christ, the hunted, the
    hated, the killed,

David's heart raced
with the fear
of being hounded.

His mouth prayed
for refuge and rescue.

And his hands preyed
on his neighbor's wife.

Your heart pounded
    with the Pharisees'
    pursuit.
Your mouth prayed
    for your cup to be
    removed.
Your hands were
    pierced all the way
    through for a crime
    you didn't do.

So now we ask
to be hounded by grace,

to be followed
and tracked
by your
relentless pursuit
in the pain we cause
and the pain we endure.

Because our hearts race,
our mouths pray,
and our hands ache
to be sought and held
by a Love
that is good
all the way through.

Amen.

Follow. Such a soft word
for a tenacious Shepherd.

I wonder how he wrote it—
as David, the hunted,
or David, the crowned.

I wonder when he decided
to flip the script on persecution,
to demote Saul's bloodthirst
to a footnote in the story
of Goodness and Love
hounding him into glory.

We are not just followed.
We are being found.

We are tracked. We are traced.
We are hunted. We are dogged.

All the harm that haunts us,
all the ways we have been chased,
they have nothing on the resolve
of God's hounding grace.

> "The one who enters by the gate is the shepherd of the sheep. The gatekeeper opens the gate for him, and the sheep listen to his voice. He calls his own sheep by name and leads them out."
>
> **JOHN 10:2-3** NIV

During the riots in Palestine in the middle of the 1930s, the British government punished an entire village by seizing their sheep and goats. Officials shut hundreds upon hundreds of animals into one big pen and told the citizens they could redeem their possessions at a price.

In the village was one orphan boy, whose tiny flock was all he had in the world for love and livelihood. He somehow scraped together enough cash to rescue his sheep and went to pay the British official at the gate. The man took the money but laughed at the boy, mocking him as he motioned at the mass of sheep and goats. Surely, it was futile—laughable even—to expect to find his few sheep in such a sea.

But the boy knew better. Raising his pipe to his lips, he sounded his distinct call. And his sheep followed him all the way home.

On the evening of that first day of the week, when the disciples were together, with the doors locked for fear of the Jewish leaders, Jesus came and stood among them and said, "Peace be with you!"
JOHN 20:19 NIV

Omnipotent Lord,

You made
doubt and death
into a doorway.

Come again
and stand with us
behind our locked doors,
where our courage
is bolted behind fear.

Because, Jesus,
your blessing of peace
is the key that turns fear
into courage's true entrance.

Amen.

You were not made to live small,
like a Post-it note of a person.

You do not have to live pressed
under the weight of someone
else's wishes, pierced by the pen
of someone else's words, inked
with the list of someone else's
needs, crumpled in the trash
when they are done using you.

You are not disposable.

Step out of the shape
you've been folded into.
Be inconvenient. Be
bulky. Be big. It is time
to unfold. It is time
to rewrite. The only words
that belong on the pages
of your life tell a story
of courage, written
with Christ.

My friend's words scraped me like a rock
when I tripped on her past
as we talked in her yard.

The scrape stung, and for a moment
I judged her as rude.
Until I remembered
the rain she's endured,
the weight of the drops,
the losses that carved her edges
but couldn't erase her rock.

And then I sat back in wonder
at the person who endured.

Jagged edges
reveal resilience
taking shape.

Next time I see a person's sharp edges,
I want to listen for the story
that is sculpting them,
expecting to see the God
who is holding them together.

May we be story-seekers.

Resurrected Lord,

you who let them
bruise your body
before rising again
on the third day:

grant us imagination to bless
even the groaning
of our bodies
as the brave beginning
of resurrection,

that in the beating
of our hearts
and the breath
within our chests
each day we would practice
the exhale of disdain
and the inhale of
the Spirit's love instead.

Amen.

"I've loved you the way my Father has loved me. Make yourselves at home in my love. If you keep my commands, you'll remain intimately at home in my love. That's what I've done—kept my Father's commands and made myself at home in his love.

"I've told you these things for a purpose: that my joy might be your joy, and your joy wholly mature."

JOHN 15:9–11 MSG

Abiding Love,

you whose trust
invited us to live
inside the home
of God's love:

restore our joy.

Because pain
has pushed us
right out the door
of trust, but your smile
can bring us to safety inside,

for you
are making
your joy
our home.

Amen.

May I learn to see
my symptoms of stress
not as proof of pathology
but as portals into God's presence.

May I bless
my soul's great refusal
to live at an inhuman pace.

May I dwell
in the home
of grace.

Lord of all color and sound,

whose word
made worlds
and whose love
makes life abound:

Paint on our hearts
indelible amber and crimson hues
of a story where death cannot refuse
to revel in the day that tombs will bloom.

Revise the couplets of our sadness and scars
that today we might sense your Love from afar.

Awaken our ears with the rhythm and tone
of Love writing our lives into a poem.

Because your word
is still making
a world of wonder
within us.

Amen.

To all whose bones
are dry, broken, and cracked:
Your throat contracts. Your skin
is chapped. Your hopes were cut
with a scriptural sword. Your trust
was scattered like dust in the wind.

We, the breathless, beg:

Can these bones live again?

Through Ezekiel God says:

When I made the world,
my Breath   made you.

I will open up the graves
        of others' grandiosity

        that swallowed you whole.
I will raise you from the ruins
        that crumbled your soul.
I will breathe my own Spirit
        into you again.

My breath   is your entrance.
My exhale   your door
    to the home others took,
    to the security that is yours.

I will give you a Shepherd
who will seek and restore
your life to my love
and your joy to be full.

    And I will never again
    leave you alone.

My magnificent refuge
now dwells   in your lungs.
Return to your breath.   Follow me home.

And I heard a loud voice from the throne saying, "Look! God's dwelling place is now among the people, and he will dwell with them. They will be his people, and God himself will be with them and be their God."

REVELATION 21:3 NIV

O Christ,

you who still sit in skin
at the side of our Father:

help me bless this body.

You did not break your body
for me to break mine.

You broke your body
to make mine blessed.

Help me see my skin
from your seat, where
every ounce of me
is loved and lovely.

And with this gaze,
I will greet
mine and all
groaning bodies
as glorious.

Amen.

I started blessing
what I had been avoiding.

Saint, in my skin.
Saint, in my sin.
Saint, in my struggle.

I started seeing
the swelling of my skin
as the story of my resilience.

I started holding
the pills in my hand
as prayers of perseverance.

I started naming
my imperfect reflection
in the mirror as ineffaceable
in glory and goodness.

This tender flesh
is chosen and always loved,
a walking miracle
of grace and grit.

All its swelling and shrinking
is but stretching

to hold the mystery
of being embraced by Jesus
and renamed as Beloved
by the Father.

Stop turning away
from what God
is always turned toward.

See your skin
and say your name:

Saint.
Saint.
Saint.

"I will ask the Father, and he will give you another advocate to help you and be with you forever—the Spirit of truth. The world cannot accept him, because it neither sees him nor knows him. But you know him, for he lives with you and will be in you."

JOHN 14:16-17 NIV

Jesus,

You promised
your Spirit
would dwell
inside us.

Rebuild
the house
of our humility.

Because so much
of our lives have
been spent trying
to build a kingdom
for you, when you
have been building
a home in us all along.

Amen.

"I am the living bread that came down from heaven. Whoever eats this bread will live forever. This bread is my flesh, which I will give for the life of the world."

JOHN 6:51 NIV

Courage is a circle.

Christ never stops
chasing us
where pain
is piercing
us through
—into communion,
into joy.

Courage is simply
the surrender to Love
—who finds you in your sin,
who seeks you in your pain,
who weeps for all the wrong
that has smeared mud over your name.

Let this Shepherd lead you into courage
with every passing day,
and freed by Christ's own scars,
may your wounds become the welcome
for those who are still chained.

All your wounds
can become
wellsprings.

"How many loaves do you have?" he asked. "Go and see."
When they found out, they said, "Five—and two fish."
MARK 6:38 NIV

Another of his disciples, Andrew, Simon Peter's brother, spoke
up, "Here is a boy with five small barley loaves and two small
fish, but how far will they go among so many?"
JOHN 6:8-9 NIV

Jesus,

you who saw abundance
where your disciples
saw lack:

help us bless
what we can offer today.

Because
every day
we are invited
to become like that kid
who showed up to listen
but was not too proud
to offer the little bit he had
to help feed the crowd.

May our cracked
yet open hands

find that abundance
is a mystery you make
when we show up
with our little loaves and fish
and expect you
to multiply grace.

Amen.

May the God of courage fill you with all you need.

Bear witness to your life, trusting you are being followed and called by the Voice of Love every day.

Receive rest as your right. May quiet waters drip you into remembrance of your baptism as one whom God always loves. When you are afraid or ashamed, may you find your breath can bring you back to life. Refuse to separate God's glory from your good. Even though valleys will stretch across your life, may you walk in wonder at how God will pave vulnerability into the intersection of sorrow and joy.

Remember that fear is only the first moment of courage, for fear is always a place Christ has visited before you and waits with you.

Look for the Shepherd's staff to rest across your shoulders as a reminder of divine presence rather than a rod of punishment.

Return to the table God keeps preparing for you. This seat and food and wine are yours regardless of those who uninvite you.

God will never leave you without a witness or a name. God anoints you not for what you've done but for who you will become.

When you have been emptied, poured out like wine, may you find you were somehow being filled.

May these words become your truth, forever your sign: *My cup overflows. In me, Love resides.*

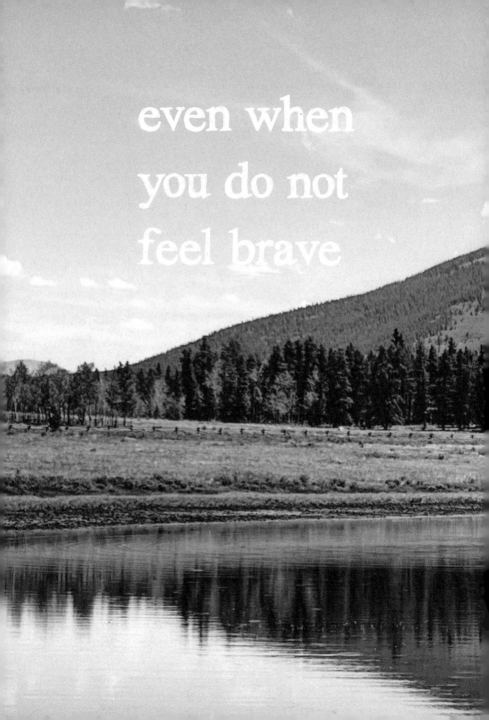